# So Many Houses

**Written by Hester Thompson Bass • Illustrated by Alik Arzoumanian**

**Children's Press®**
A Division of Scholastic Inc.
New York • Toronto • London • Auckland • Sydney
Mexico City • New Delhi • Hong Kong
Danbury, Connecticut

*To Helen Thompson, who gave me a love of words*
H.B.

*For Varak*
A. A.


**Reading Consultant**

Eileen Robinson
Reading Specialist

Library of Congress Cataloging-in-Publication Data

Bass, Hester, 1956–
So many houses / written by Hester Bass ; illustrated by Alik Arzoumanian.
  p. cm. — (A rookie reader)
ISBN 0-516-24977-0 (lib. bdg.)      0-516-24999-1 (pbk.)
1. Dwellings—Juvenile literature. I. Arzoumanian, Alik. II. Title. III. Series.
TH4811.5.B38 2006
728'.3—dc22

                                    2005016149

CHILDREN'S PRESS, and A ROOKIE READER®, and associated logos are trademarks and/or
registered trademarks of Scholastic Library Publishing. SCHOLASTIC and associated logos are
trademarks and/or registered trademarks of Scholastic Inc.
1 2 3 4 5 6 7 8 9 10 R 15 14 13 12 11 10 09 08 07 06

There are so many houses
around the world.

A house made of logs.

A house made of bricks.

A house made of rocks.

A house made of sticks.

A house made of mud.

A house made of snow.

Apartment houses.
Row after row.

A house in a car.

19

A house made of glass.

A house in a tree.

A house made of grass.

A house on a mountain.

A house by the sea.

Which house is best
for your family?

# WORD LIST (36 Words)

(Words in **bold** are story words that are repeated throughout the text.)

| | | | |
|---|---|---|---|
| **a** | family | **made** | snow |
| after | for | many | so |
| are | glass | mountain | sticks |
| around | grass | mud | the |
| apartment | **house** | **of** | there |
| best | houses | on | tree |
| bricks | in | rocks | which |
| by | is | row | world |
| car | logs | sea | your |

## About the Author

A librarian's daughter, Hester Bass imagines books as tickets to anywhere in the world. Hester enjoys traveling and has visited many of the kinds of houses in this book. She lives with her family in a house made of wood and glass at the foot of a mountain in Alabama.

## About the Illustrator

Alik Arzoumanian creates her illustrations from an orange room, in a small apartment, in a red brick building in Cambridge, Massachusetts.